AF271185

CATERPILLAR D-8
1933 THROUGH 1974

Including Diesel Seventy-Five and RD-8
PHOTO ARCHIVE

Bob LaVoie

Iconografix
Photo Archive Series

Iconografix
PO Box 446
Hudson, Wisconsin 54016 USA

© 1999 by Bob LaVoie

All rights reserved. No part of this work may be reproduced or used in any form by any means... graphic, electronic, or mechanical, including photocopying, recording, taping, or any other information storage and retrieval system... without written permission of the publisher.

The information in this book is true and complete to the best of our knowledge. All recommendations are made without any guarantee on the part of the author or Publisher, who also disclaim any liability incurred in connection with the use of this data or specific details.

We acknowledge that certain words, such as model names and designations, mentioned herein are the property of the trademark holder. We use them for purposes of identification only. This is not an official publication.

Iconografix books are offered at a discount when sold in quantity for promotional use. Businesses or organizations seeking details should write to the Marketing Department, Iconografix, at the above address.

Library of Congress Card Number: 98-75276

ISBN 1-882256-96-4

99 00 01 02 03 04 05 5 4 3 2 1

Printed in the United States of America

Cover and book design by Shawn Glidden
Edited Dylan Frautschi

PREFACE

The histories of machines and mechanical gadgets are contained in the books, journals, correspondence, and personal papers stored in libraries and archives throughout the world. Written in tens of languages, covering thousands of subjects, the stories are recorded in millions of words.

Words are powerful. Yet, the impact of a single image, a photograph or an illustration, often relates more than dozens of pages of text. Fortunately, many of the libraries and archives that house the words also preserve the images.

In the *Photo Archive Series,* Iconografix reproduces photographs and illustrations selected from public and private collections. The images are chosen to tell a story—to capture the character of their subject. Reproduced as found, they are accompanied by the captions made available by the archive.

The Iconografix *Photo Archive Series* is dedicated to young and old alike, the enthusiast, the collector and anyone who, like us, is fascinated by "things" mechanical.

Iconografix Inc. exists to preserve history through the publication of notable photographic archives and the list of titles under the Iconografix imprint is constantly growing. Transportation enthusiasts should be on the Iconografix mailing list and are invited to write and ask for a catalog, free of charge.

Authors and editors in the field of transportation history are invited to contact the Editorial Department at Iconografix, Inc., PO Box 446, Hudson, WI 54016. We require a minimum of 120 photographs per subject. We prefer subjects narrow in focus, e.g., a specific model, railroad, or racing venue. Photographs must be of high-quality, suited to large format reproduction.

Dedication

This book is dedicated to my long time friend and mentor Larry Palecek. Thank you for the guidance and friendship over all these years, and the pleasure of push loading that beautiful old 2U "big Molly" and her #80 for the last time....

Willis Rowe of Bloomington, IL, uses his Diesel Seventy-Five to pull a scraper. Pictured here in September 1933 working at Carlock, IL, to divert a creek channel.

INTRODUCTION

The origin of the D-8 tractor of today began in 1904 with the first practical gas powered crawler tractor. Later, in 1925 with the newly formed Caterpillar Tractor Company, interest began to move toward perfecting diesel power in the crawler tractor.

In 1931 it happened. A gas 60 tractor was fitted with a D9900 engine and the diesel Caterpillar was born. Production of the historic 1C series diesel 60 and 65 tractors was followed closely by the company and competitors alike. Later, in 1933, the 3C Diesel 70 would be fitted with the same 4 cylinder D9900 engine. It was a success in a big way. No longer was the large-scale farmer or contractor faced with high fuel bills and frequent engine rebuilds. Now he had durable, low cost, power to master his fields, road projects, and quarries.

It would be five years or so before the smaller farmer had the benefit of diesel power. But as he waited, new styles of tractors with massive 6 cylinder engines were rolling off the Peoria assembly lines. First, on April 24, 1933, came the 2E series Diesel Seventy-Five. Weighing 32,600 lbs with 83 drawbar horsepower, this was the great grand father of the D-8 making his debut. Production ended October 28, 1935 with 1,105 tractors produced.

Next came the RD-8 – the RD designating either Rudolf Diesel, Rosen Diesel (for Art Rosen, inventor of the D9900 Caterpillar Diesel engine), or Roosevelt Diesel (for President Roosevelt), depending on which version of the story you believe. Given the serial number prefix 1H and 5E, production began January 31, 1935. The last of the true RD-8 tractors came at number 1H2409. With machine 1H2410, the D-8 was born.

Caterpillar went on to make many changes in the D-8 to get to the elevated sprocket, tiller controlled differential steer machines like today's D-8R. Here is a list of D-8 tractors and former models by model, serial number and year.

HISTORY OF D-8 AND ITS PREDECESSORS

Model		Serial	Year	Drive
Diesel 70		3E (D9900)	1933	
Diesel 75		2E	1933	
RD-8		5E8001& 1H	1935	
D-8		1H2409	1937	
D-8		8R	1941	
D-8		2U	1945	
D-8		13A	1953	
D-8	F	14A	1955	direct drive
D-8	F	14A3861	1956	direct drive
D-8	D	15A	1955	torque converter
D-8	G	15A1673	1956	torque converter
D-8	H	35A	1959	torque converter
D-8	H	36A	1958	direct drive
D-8	H	46A	1959	power shift
D-8	K	76V	1974	direct drive

Acknowledgments

I wish to thank the Caterpillar Inc. Business Resource Center for helping me obtain images from the Corporate archives. I also owe sincere gratitude to Dick Ryan, Gresham, Oregon, for the technical advice for this project. And as always, to my wife Heather for her continuing help and support for my hobby.

Working in California in 1938, a Diesel Seventy-Five equipped with front brush guard and towing a Hyster tracked arch skids a redwood to the landing.

Working at Mendota, CA, this Diesel Seventy-Five pulls an Oliver 18 disk plow, covering a 240" swath at 2 mph in red adobe soil. They cover 100 acres per 20 hour day on less than 4 gallons of fuel an hour.

A newly painted Diesel Seventy-Five awaits shipping outside of a Peoria plant. Notice the twin front idlers which were standard on the Diesel Seventy-Five and the early RD-8 tractors.

Towing a Fowler 4-bottom plow in Northern France, a Diesel Seventy-Five works in August 1933.

Diesel Seventy-Five with Hyster winch towing a tracked Hyster logging arch.

A model Diesel Seventy-Five leads a tracked convoy in peace time Military operations.

This Diesel Seventy-Five is equipped with a re-enforced front radiator guard with skid pan and swinging front tow hook. May 1933.

A Diesel Seventy-Five fitted with optional lighting group, canopy and tow hook, sitting outside of a Peoria plant.

A Diesel Seventy-Five with skeleton street pads that will accept bolt-on ice or dirt cleats. It has been fitted with louvered engine side doors. The square dash is part of the engine door option.

A model Seventy-Five snow special equipped with snow and ice pads, fully enclosed cab lighting group and battery box.

Working on the Pacific Highway near Sylvina, WA, a Diesel Seventy-Five pulling a 12 yard scraper, works 2 shifts in February 1936.

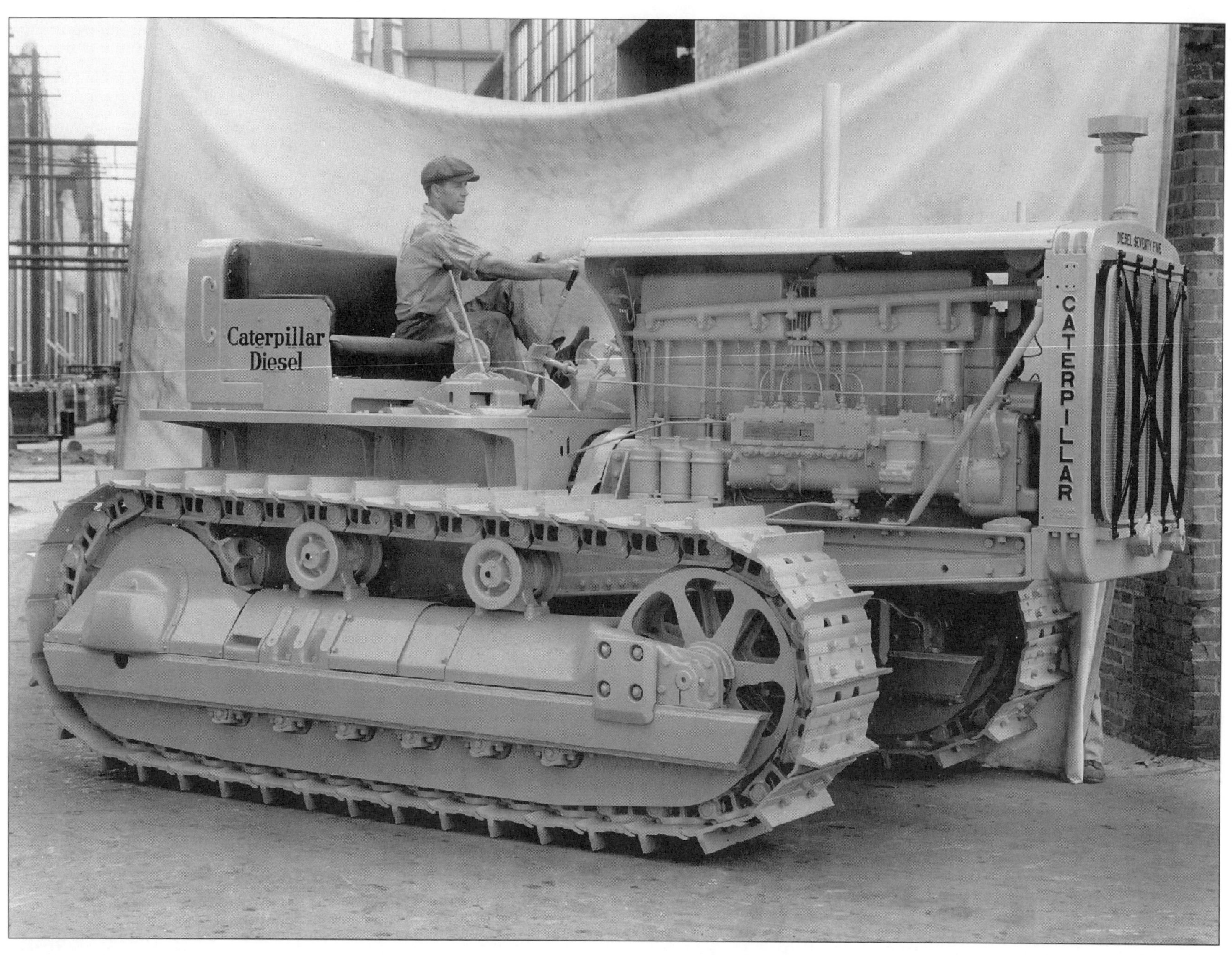

A standard equipped Diesel Seventy-Five is operated into position by a factory worker for a photo.

A Model Seventy-Five outside a Peoria factory, equipped with a 3 shank rear mounted sub-soiler. Also notice the pan-type attachments bolted to the track shoe for use on flat surfaces or streets.

A Diesel Seventy-Five with front brush guard, skid pan and enclosed cab sits parked outside a Peoria factory. This machine seems to be set up for logging or forestry type work in extremely cold areas.

A Diesel Seventy-Five with a rear mounted cable control unit and angle dozer blade works in a quarry in Northern Minnesota.

A factory photo of the 6 cylinder engine used in the later Diesel Seventy-Five and early D-8.

MASTER FILE
DO NOT REMOVE

"Caterpillar" Diesel Seventy-Five Tractor

[SPECIFICATIONS ON OTHER SIDE]

SPECIFICATIONS
"CATERPILLAR" DIESEL SEVENTY-FIVE

Capacity, maximum at sea level—

(As there has been as yet no opportunity to make an official test at the University of Nebraska, the values are computed for maximum load, corrected to sea level barometric pressure and the standard temperature of 60° F., in accordance with correction calculations outlined in the A.S.A.E. and S.A.E. test code. This correction brings all horsepower and drawbar values to the one common basis of comparison recognized by the engineering profession.)

Drawbar horsepower	80
Belt horsepower	93

Drawbar pull in pounds:

First	18100
Second	13060
Third	10960
Fourth	9160
Fifth	7340
Sixth	4870
Reverse—low	18100
Reverse—high	10960

Drawbar pull, maximum, in pounds. When slowed down by overload, "Caterpillar" engines develop a considerably greater turning effort at the flywheel (torque), which results in greater drawbar pull at reduced travel speed:

First	19625
Second	14160
Third	11890
Fourth	9930
Fifth	7960
Sixth	5280
Reverse—low	19625
Reverse—high	11890

Speeds in M.P.H. at full load governed engine R.P.M.

First	1.7
Second	2.3
Third	2.7
Fourth	3.1
Fifth	3.7
Sixth	5.0
Reverse—low	1.7
Reverse—high	2.7

Engine—four cycle, water cooled:

Fuel	Commerc'l Diesel Oil
Number of cylinders	6
Bore and stroke, in inches	5¼x8
Piston displacement, in cubic inches	1039
R.P.M.—governed, at full load	820

Piston speed, in feet per minute	1093
R.P.M. at maximum drawbar pull (point of maximum torque)	600
N.A.C.C. horsepower rating for tax purposes	66.15
Lubrication	Force Feed

Crankshaft:

Number of main bearings	7
Diameter of main bearings, in inches	3½
Total area main bearing surface, in sq. inches	200
Gauge (center to center tracks), in inches	78
Length of tracks on ground (center drive sprocket to center front idler), in inches	97⅝
Area ground contact (with standard track shoes), in sq. inches	3515

Overall:

Length, in inches	183
Height (measured from tip of grouser of standard track shoe to highest point, exclusive of exhaust and intake pipe), in inches	84⅛
Width, in inches	103¾
Ground clearance (measured from lower face of standard track shoe), in inches	10½
Height drawbar above ground (measured from lower face of standard track shoe), in inches	17½
Lateral movement drawbar (measured at pin), in inches	43

Track:

Width of standard track shoe, in inches	18
Height of grouser (measured from upper face of standard track shoe), in inches	2¹⁹/₃₂
Diameter of track shoe bolts, in inches	¾
Diameter of track pins, in inches	1¾
Diameter of track pin bushings, in inches	2¾

Steering.......Each track controlled by slow speed heavy duty dry multiple disk clutch and contracting band brake

Plates in each steering clutch:

Number	30
Friction area each plate, in sq. inches	66
Total friction surface, in sq. inches	1980

Transmission.......Power transmitted through dry type flywheel clutch to selective type change speed gear set

Capacities:

Cooling system, in U. S. Standard gallons	28

Lubricating system:

Crank case, in quarts	28
Transmission case, in quarts	40
Final drive case (each), in quarts	26
Fuel tank, in U. S. Standard gallons	99
Weight, shipping (approximate), in pounds	30550

CATERPILLAR TRACTOR CO.
PEORIA, ILLINOIS, U. S. A.
Track-type Tractors » Combines » Road Machinery

THERE IS A "CATERPILLAR" DEALER NEAR YOU

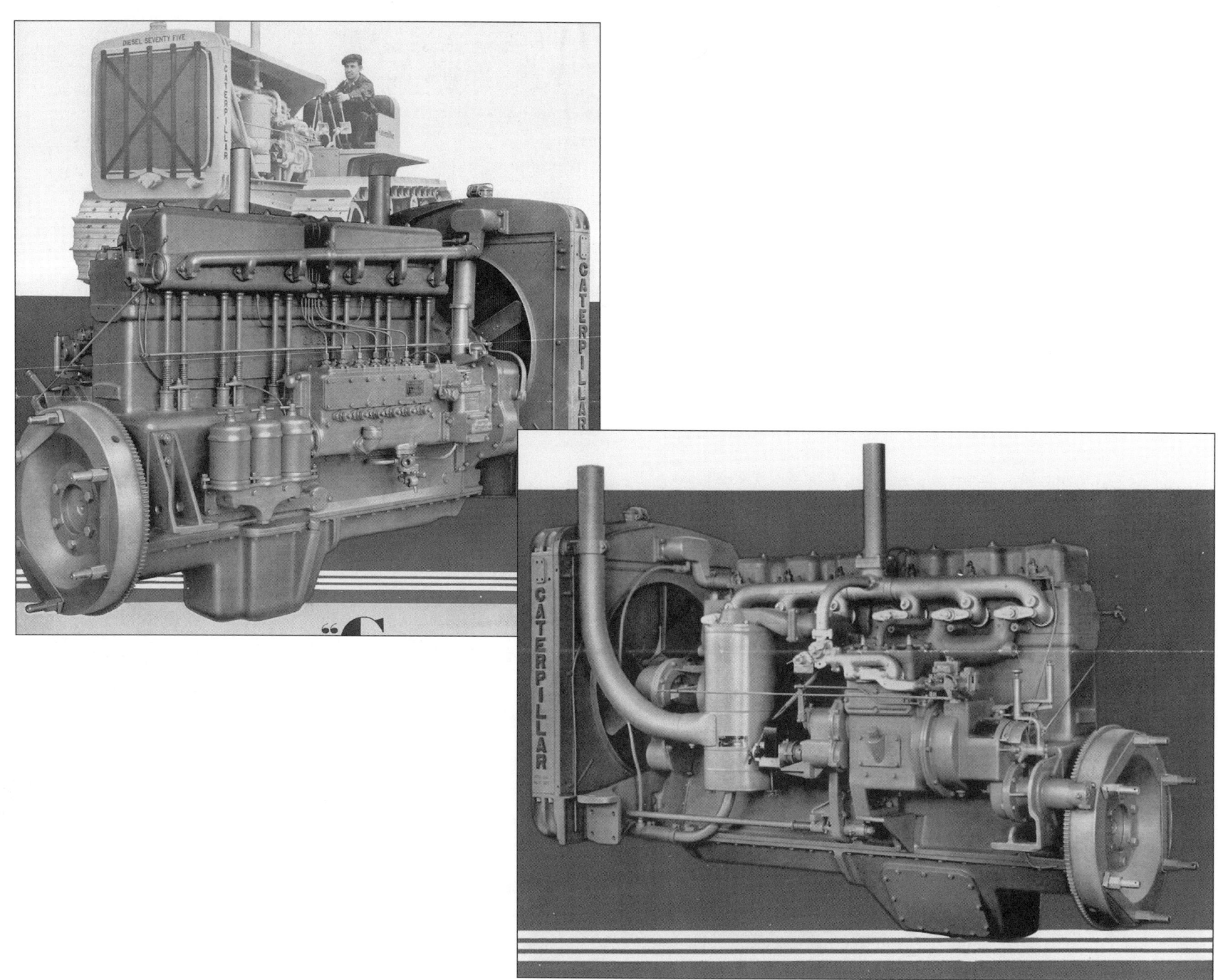

The Ten-Thousandth "Caterpillar" Diesel

» *President B. C. Heacock of Caterpillar Tractor Co. Attaches the Production Tag to the 10,000th "Caterpillar" Diesel.*

PEORIA, ILLINOIS, Nov. 13. 1935.—The completion of one of the tractors in today's assembly line marked an important event—the engine that powered it was the 10,000th "Caterpillar" Diesel. Its predecessors are at work in every State in the United States, every Province in Canada, and in 71 other countries—great and constantly growing evidence of successful and satisfying performance.

The Complete "CATERPILLAR" Line

"Caterpillar" Tractors are available in sizes ranging from 80 to 18 maximum drawbar horsepower. Six are gasoline powered—three are Diesel powered.

Six sizes of "Caterpillar" Blade Graders—four of the leaning wheel type weighing from 12,020 pounds to 5,420 pounds with standard blades from 12 feet to 8 feet—two of the straight wheel type with 7-foot blades, weighing 3,720 pounds and 2,978 pounds.

Three sizes of "Caterpillar" Auto Patrols with 12-foot blade as standard equipment, range in weight from 14,350 pounds to 10,968 pounds. A "Caterpillar" Hi-way Patrol with standard 8-foot blade weighing 1,376 pounds. "Caterpillar" Trailer Patrol with 12-foot blade, available with any of four combinations of power and hand control, weighing from 5,728 pounds to 5,120 pounds.

"Caterpillar" Elevating Grader—equipped with "Caterpillar" Power Unit for carrier drive.

"Caterpillar" Power Units and Industrial Engines range in size from 102 to 36 maximum brake horsepower. Available as engine alone as well as in complete Power Units with engine, radiator, fuel tank and clutch compactly mounted on steel skids.

Three sizes of "Caterpillar" combines with header lengths ranging from 20 feet to 10 feet. Available for level land or medium hillside operation and equipped with bulk grain tank or sacking equipment. Various equipment available for harvesting a wide range of crops.

Various "Caterpillar" Agricultural Implements include: "Caterpillar" Terracer with 8-foot blade, weighing 1,410 pounds; two multiple implement hitches with maximum distance between implement couplings ranging from 42 feet to 12 feet; "Caterpillar" Mower with 7-foot cut; and "Caterpillar" Push Rake with a 13-foot sweep.

A SIZE FOR EVERY USE

RECEIVED
PATENT DEPT.
MAY 22 1933
CATERPILLAR TRACTOR CO.

FORM 1963

PRINTED IN U.S.A.

30

ROAD BUILDING . . . . 35 to 40 gallons of 7 cent fuel a day are used by this Diesel Seventy-Five to pull the "Caterpillar" Elevating Grader. A fuel cost of only $2.50 to $2.80 per 10-hour day—25c to 28c per hour.

AGRICULTURE . . . Pulling three 9-foot one-way disk plows in fourth gear and covering 180 acres every 24 hours. Fuel consumption is 4½ gallons of 3 cent fuel per hour—a fuel cost of 13½c per hour—less than 2c per acre.

EARTH MOVING . . . Moving 600 cubic yards of sand per 12-hour day on a 500-foot haul. Using 5 gallons of 6½ cent fuel per hour. Total fuel cost is 32½ cents an hour—less than ⅔ of a cent per cubic yard.

LOGGING . . . 25 to 30 gallons of Diesel fuel per 8-hour day with fuel costing 5 cents a gallon—a total fuel cost of 16c to 19c an hour.

31

Here're Two!

The horse (lower right) wonders how anything can "work so much and eat so little" as it watches this Diesel Seventy-Five and Diesel Fifty on a Federal Highway contract of J. J. Dooling at Gillette, Wyoming.

First 3—then 14—now 21!

Dick-Smith Eng. Co., and A. E. Dick Construction Co., affiliated coal-stripping contractors at Hazelton, Pennsylvania first bought 3 "Caterpillar" Diesel Tractors—they now own 14. They also operate 7 shovels powered by "Caterpillar" Diesel Engines.

10 en route—5 at home!

Ten "Caterpillar" Diesel Seventy-Fives are changed from boat to flatcars to continue their trip to a large estate in the Dutch East Indies —where five more are working.

Quintuplets!

Brimful is the way these "Caterpillar" Diesel Seventy-Fives like their loads on this O'Meara Construction Co. job at Quincy, Illinois. They own three more!

1+2+4 = 7 "Caterpillar" Diesels

"Hustle along" says this Diesel Seventy-Five to six other "Caterpillar" Diesel Tractors as it keeps another member of the family busy—the "Caterpillar" Elevating Grader. This 100% "Caterpillar" meeting is held by Birt Bros. at Decatur, Illinois.

Three and One !

At Grand Coulee Dam, Rowland Construction Co., of Seattle, Washington work three of their four "Caterpillar" Diesel Tractors 20 hours per day. Big loads! Low costs! Steady service! Simple operation!—four good reasons why this concern owns four "Caterpillar" Diesel Tractors.

First 3 — then 14 — now 21 !

Dick-Smith Eng. Co., and A. E. Dick Construction Co., affiliated coal-stripping contractors at Hazelton, Pennsylvania first bought 3 "Caterpillar" Diesel Tractors—they now own 14. They also operate 7 shovels powered by "Caterpillar" Diesel Engines.

Three Pair !

Down on the levee, "Caterpillar" Diesel Tractors are boosting "Mississippi mud" on the Mike Morrissey contract near White Hall Landing, Arkansas. This user owns 6 "Caterpillar" Diesel Tractors.

Lubrication · A pressure lubrication system provides positive lubrication of the vital parts of the Seventy-Five Engine. The oil pump, driven off the cam shaft, combines both scavenging and pumping units. The two scavenging units draw the oil from the ends of the crank case through large surface screens and deliver it into the oil sump. The pressure unit draws the oil from the sump through another large surface screen, and delivers it under approximately 30 pounds pressure to the crankshaft bearings, connecting rod bearings, piston pin bearings, valve rocker arm mechanism, the front cam shaft bearing, fan shaft, and the upper oil pump shaft bearing. Three large capacity lubricant filters continuously clean the oil as it leaves the oil pump, removing foreign material that would otherwise reach the working parts of the engine. These filters are mounted on the outside of the cylinder block where they are easily accessible for cleaning. In case a filter becomes clogged, the oil is by-passed, so that lubrication is not interrupted.

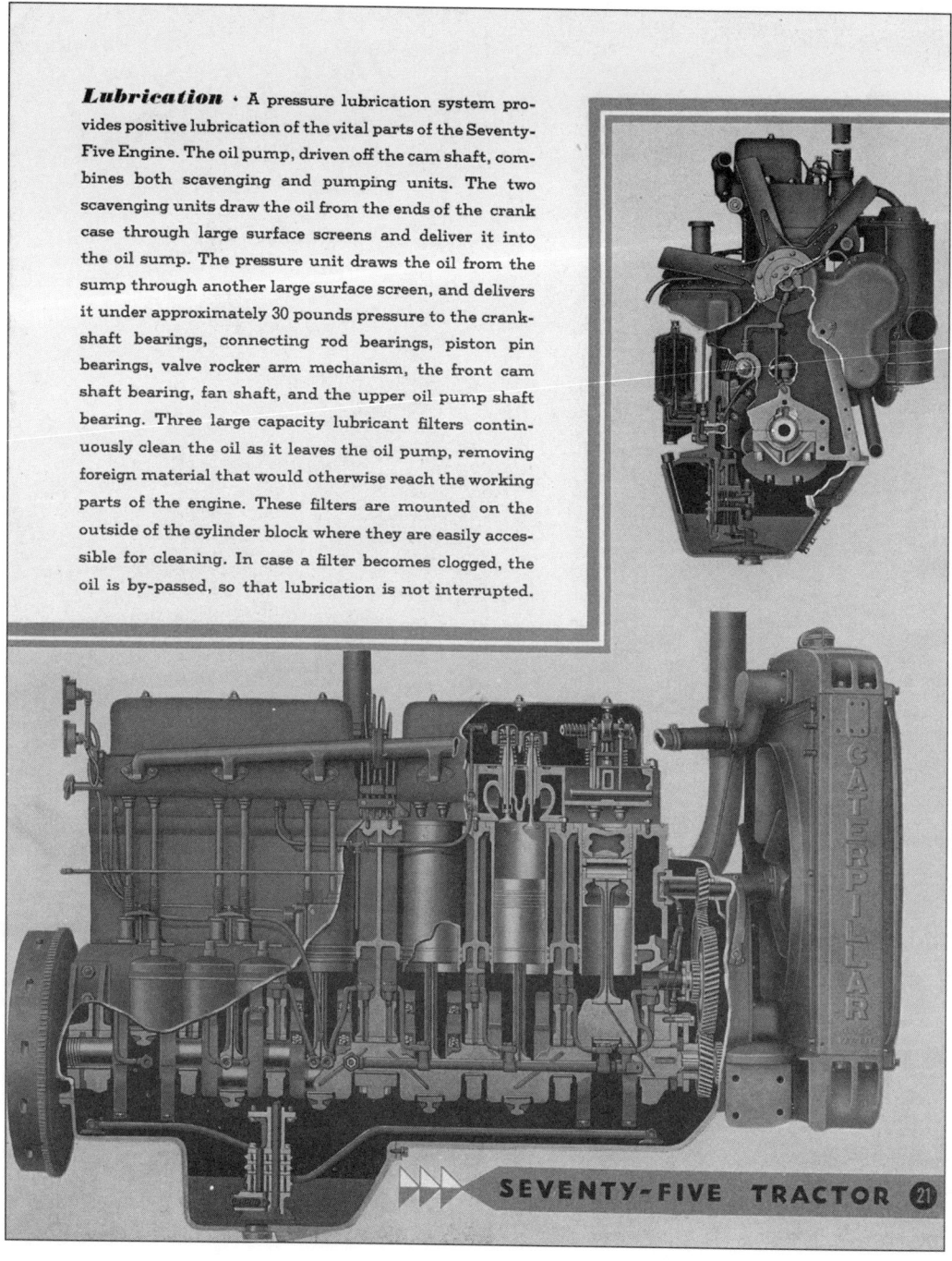

SEVENTY-FIVE TRACTOR 21

Continuous, dependable power for starting is supplied by this starting engine—a two cylinder four-cycle gasoline engine of "Caterpillar" design and manufacture.

Starting Equipment ‧ Positive starting of the "Caterpillar" Diesel Seventy-Five Engine under all climatic conditions is assured by the use of a small two-cylinder auxiliary "Caterpillar" gasoline engine mounted on the left side of the cylinder block. The starting unit is started by a hand crank at the front of the radiator. It turns over the Diesel engine through a starter gear that engages a ring gear on the flywheel. As soon as the Diesel operates under its own power, the starter gear automatically disengages.

Starting of the "Caterpillar" Diesel Seventy-Five is further facilitated by employing heat from the starting engine to warm up the Diesel and speed up the starting operation. The control of this heating is manually adjustable to meet varying climatic conditions.

The use of an independent small gasoline engine for starting the "Caterpillar" Diesel was adopted after wide observation and experimentation with all available starting methods. It avoids complication of design of the Diesel engine, provides a unit that is simple, dependable and that can continue to turn over the Diesel engine as long as may be necessary.

SEVENTY-FIVE TRACTOR 23

and dependable service. "Caterpillar" Tractors are called upon to work in dust and mud and sand—successful operation under such conditions calls for effective means of keeping the oil in and the dirt out of gears and bearings. The seals at this point are of the bellows-type—close-fitting, self-aligning, self-adjusting. Smooth, hardened, corrosion-resistant washers fit on each side of the final drive sprocket —against these washers the flat cork sealing surfaces of the copper bellows seal are pressed by a series of coil springs. Oil inside the bellows lubricates the rubbing surfaces and works outward between them to carry dirt away from the outer edges. Because its effectiveness does not depend upon high pressure, this seal wastes no power—because it is flexible, it maintains its effectiveness without necessity of adjustment.

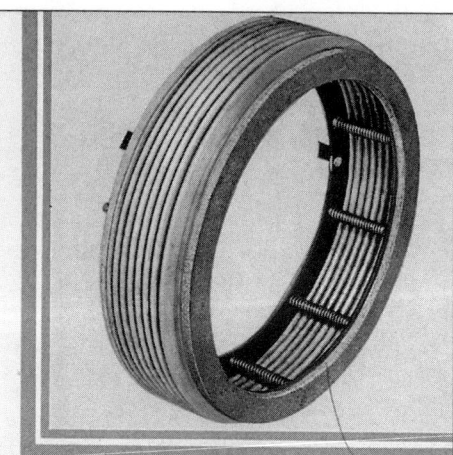

One of the metal bellows type, flexible dust seals that protect the final drive mechanism. The flexibility and expansion of these seals, actuated by springs, provide maximum protection for the vital parts of the final drive mechanism. The seals never require adjustment.

▶▶▶ SEVENTY-FIVE TRACTOR ㉛

Equalizer Spring · The weight of the engine and transmission assemblies is transmitted to the track roller frames through the sprocket shaft at the rear and the equalizer spring at the front. The equalizer spring is mounted under the engine rear support—its ends rest in brackets on the two track roller frames. This massive steel spring is correctly proportioned to combine strength for severe service with resiliency to cushion shocks. Its mounting permits the spring to tilt in either direction so that the tracks can oscillate—two supplementary leaf springs retain and permit maximum oscillation of the equalizer spring. The equalizer spring has only the function of bearing weight—it has no additional burden of keeping track roller frames in alignment.

The track roller frames are free to oscillate vertically when the front end of either track runs up on a bank, rock or stump—the equalizer spring tilts and flexes—twist and strain are not communicated to the transmission and engine.

Special Equipment

(SUPPLIED AT EXTRA COST)

The standard "Caterpillar" Diesel Seventy-Five Tractor is regularly equipped to meet the requirements of a wide range of operating conditions and jobs. However, to meet the requirements of those conditions and jobs of a more unusual nature, certain items of special equipment are offered at a moderate extra cost for installation either at the "Caterpillar" factory or in the field. Following is a list of these items and the service for which they are intended.

Front Bumper, Radiator Guard and Engine Guard

Arrester, Spark · When using the tractor in places where the fire hazard is extraordinarily high, the spark arrester can be installed on the exhaust pipe as a safeguard against the possibility of flying sparks.

Belt Pulley Drive · By means of the belt pulley drive, the engine can be used for operating certain belt driven equipment. The belt pulley drive runs at 694 R.P.M. It is offered either without pulley or with pulley of 13-inch face and 14⁷⁄₁₆-inch diameter. Belt speed with above pulley is approximately 2,600 f.p.m. Other size pulleys can be accommodated.

Bumper, Front · A one-inch steel plate bumper, mounted directly to the structural frame of the tractor and extending to each side, serves two purposes: first, as a protection from young trees and undergrowth, and second, as a bumper for pushing heavy loads.

Cab · A snug, fully enclosed cab to protect the tractor operator from the elements. Provided with sliding doors on each side and adjustable windows front and rear.

Curtains, for Canopy Top · Curtains are offered for use with those Diesel Seventy-Fives equipped with canopy top. The curtains allow visibility in all directions and can be easily removed or rolled up out of the way when not in use.

Guard, Crank Case · A heavy sheet steel crankcase guard offered as protection for the crankcase against damage by rocks, stumps, etc.

Guard, Engine · Two steel plates, reinforced and attached to the tractor frame and radiator, are offered as protection for both sides of the engine. Openings in the sides of the guards permit access to parts requiring inspection. Two additional guards, for use with the

Crank Case Guard

crankcase guard, consist of triangular steel plates that attach to the crankcase guard to completely shield the engine crankcase.

Guard, Radiator · A heavy mill plate guard to protect the radiator from brush and trees. Mounted on the front bumper, and rigidly braced.

Front Pull Hook

Hook, Front Pull · A heavy hook for attachment to the front end of the tractor for pulling loads in reverse gear and for using the tractor in tandem hitch.

Lighting Equipment, Electric · Powerful headlights with brackets and necessary wiring can be installed at the "Caterpillar" factory or in the field. Equipment is offered in two types—one with current supplied direct from a generator—the other with current supplied from generator and battery.

Muffler · When desired or required by law to reduce the sound of the open exhaust, a muffler can be installed on the exhaust pipe.

Odometer · When it is desired to keep accurate work or cost records, an odometer can be installed that registers distance traveled, in miles.

Painting · The tractor is regularly supplied painted Hi-Way Yellow. Any other colors can be furnished at moderate extra cost.

Top, Canopy · A curved plate top supported by tubular uprights is offered for installation on the Diesel Seventy-five as protection for the operator against the elements.

Canopy Top

Tracks · Available track equipment aside from the standard 18-inch grouser track shoes includes: 20-inch, 22-inch and 24-inch grouser track shoes; 18-inch and 22-inch heat-treated grouser track shoes; 18-inch flat track shoes; and 18-inch skeleton track shoes.

Available grousers include: ice and dirt grousers for 18- or 22-inch grouser track shoes; dirt grousers for 18-inch flat track shoes; and ice grousers for 18-inch flat or skeleton track shoes.

Street plates are available for use with the 18-, 20-, 22- or 24-inch grouser track shoes. These plates bolt to the grouser shoes and provide a flat ground contact without projecting grousers or bolt heads.

▶▶▶ **SEVENTY-FIVE TRACTOR** 43

It's as simple as getting a coat of Olive Drab paint instead of Highway Yellow, for standard "Caterpillar" Machines to go to war. These machines have been developed through more than 37 years, to beat jobs as tough as this toughest of wars can muster!

Operating in deep forest mud, this bulldozer equipped Diesel D8 finds the traction to ram a logging road through dense tree and brush growth. Military supply lines are pushed over wooded terrain with this same outfit!

This looks like an ice-plant, for the D13000 engine is powering a compound compressor. Actually it's a forgeshop, making crankshafts and other parts for war machines, in an eastern unit of Democracy's Arsenal.

6

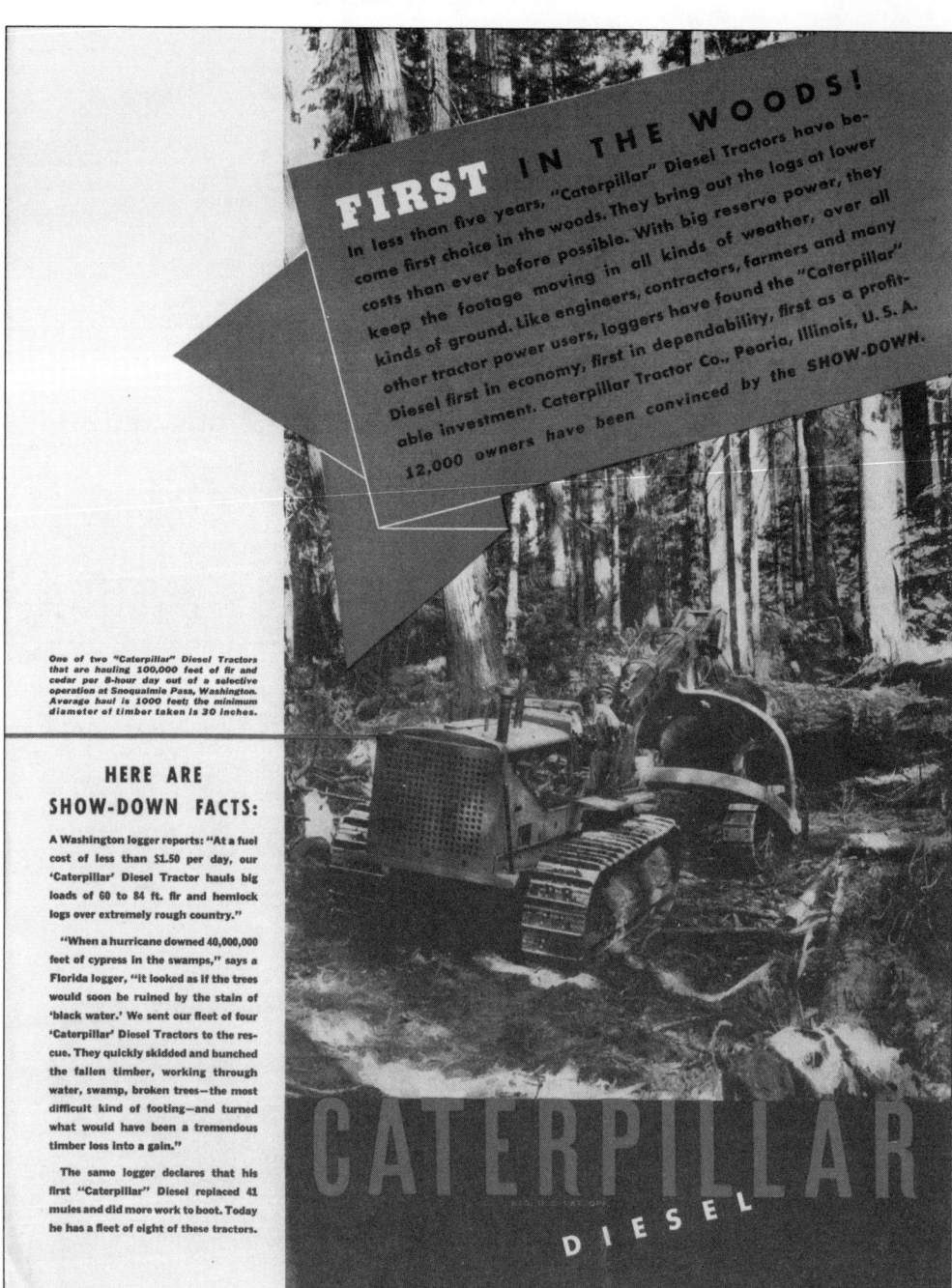

FIRST IN THE WOODS!

In less than five years, "Caterpillar" Diesel Tractors have become first choice in the woods. They bring out the logs at lower costs than ever before possible. With big reserve power, they keep the footage moving in all kinds of weather, over all kinds of ground. Like engineers, contractors, farmers and many other tractor power users, loggers have found the "Caterpillar" Diesel first in economy, first in dependability, first as a profitable investment. Caterpillar Tractor Co., Peoria, Illinois, U.S.A. 12,000 owners have been convinced by the SHOW-DOWN.

One of two "Caterpillar" Diesel Tractors that are hauling 100,000 feet of fir and cedar per 8-hour day out of a selective operation at Snoqualmie Pass, Washington. Average haul is 1000 feet; the minimum diameter of timber taken is 30 inches.

HERE ARE SHOW-DOWN FACTS:

A Washington logger reports: "At a fuel cost of less than $1.50 per day, our 'Caterpillar' Diesel Tractor hauls big loads of 60 to 84 ft. fir and hemlock logs over extremely rough country."

"When a hurricane downed 40,000,000 feet of cypress in the swamps," says a Florida logger, "it looked as if the trees would soon be ruined by the stain of 'black water.' We sent our fleet of four 'Caterpillar' Diesel Tractors to the rescue. They quickly skidded and bunched the fallen timber, working through water, swamp, broken trees—the most difficult kind of footing—and turned what would have been a tremendous timber loss into a gain."

The same logger declares that his first "Caterpillar" Diesel replaced 41 mules and did more work to boot. Today he has a fleet of eight of these tractors.

CATERPILLAR DIESEL

1936 magazine advertisement showing the advantages of Caterpillar Diesel Power in logging applications.

An RD-8 with cable blade and headlights removes snow from a downtown Milwaukee street.

An RD-8 pulling a tracked Athey wagon is loaded by a Bucyrus Erie shovel while excavating for a factory in Cleveland, OH.

September 1937, an RD-8 with a tracked side dump wagon unloads rock on a Pittsburg construction site.

March 3, 1939. The 50,000th Caterpillar Diesel rolls off the assembly line in Peoria, IL.

Commemorating the 50,000th Diesel with a soap stone pencil. Peoria, IL, March 3, 1939.

Factory photo of RD-8 tractor. Note the RD-8 identification plaque at the bottom of the radiator side rather than the top of the radiator tank. Note also the newer, smaller fuel pump.

Factory photo of a D-8, 2U series.

Harry T. Campbell and Sons of Towson, MD working on an extension of the Mt. Vernon Highway at Washington D.C. July 1936.

Two RD-8s with factory canopies and brush guards pull tracked dump wagons out of a muddy quarry in central Illinois.

An early D-8 with a cable operated blade bulldozes while pulling a compactor on a Montana road job.

52

A D-8 tractor equipped with headlights on the front cover of a 1947 sales brochure.

Factory photo of an early D-8 with hydraulic 8A bulldozer.

54

Soldier operating an early D-8 and cable operated scraper waves to airplanes in a classic W.W.II photo.

A D-8 pushes dirt over a burning B-29 in Saipan, Japan.

This D-8 equipped with cable operated blade and rear control unit pushes material off of a stock pile in a Kentucky crushing operation.

Rear view of a D-8 working on top of a stock pile with rear mounted cable control unit and straight blade.

Construction Company pulling a cable operated scraper behind an RD-8 while working on an airport runway project.

A W.W.II vintage D-8 builds a ramp for a Navy LST (landing ship tank) to unload its cargo on a South Pacific island.

A D-8 clearing palm trees for an air strip on the island of Guam during W.W.II.

A D-8 and #80 scraper loads in a sandy area at Whittier, CA, 1949.

Inside the United States Army's school of crawler tractor repair where essential field maintenance methods are taught by Caterpillar factory instructors.

A D-8 pulls stumps with a Hyster towing winch on a pipe line job for the Wunderlich and Griffis Pipe Line Construction Company of Tulsa, OK.

Three D-8 side boom equipped tractors set pipe on an Oklahoma pipe line job.

A D-7 and D-8 level sand on the Pacific island of Aniwetok in the Marshall island group for a future air strip.

Three D-8s move a large pipe section up a steep embankment on a construction project.

65486

Four D-8 tractors carry a length of pipe to be set in a trench on an Oklahoma pipe line job.

Side boom equipped D-8s owned by Wunderlich and Griffis Pipe Line Construction Company, lower pipe into a trench dug by a clam ditcher working ahead of them.

Factory photo of an early D-8 fitted with a rear cable control unit and angle blade.

A D-8 with rear mounted push block push loads a DW21 scraper in 1953.

Factory photo of a D-8 tractor with cable operated straight blade. Notice the solid front idlers which became standard with earlier 2U series tractors.

Parson and Fife Construction Company of Brigham, UT, uses a D-8 with 8S bulldozer to feed a crusher at Bonneville. Moving 250 tons per hour, gravel passes the strongest test for cement specifications without washing.

Koshak Brothers Construction of Park Falls, WI, works on the Highway 29 interchange at Wausau, WI. Peterson Construction Company's D-8 push loads Koshak's 2U and #80 scraper.

Factory photo of early model D-8 with 8S dozer and front mounted cable control unit.

Working near Joplin, MO, in 1956, a D-8 push loads a #80 scraper.

Factory view of early model D-8 with 8A dozer and front mounted cable control unit.

May 30, 1956. A pair of Caterpillar D-8 tractors pulling #80 Cat scrapers strip overburden at a mine near Sugar Grove, VA.

Chile Exploration Company uses a D-8 tractor and bulldozer to clear rock before laying track at a copper mine in October of 1949.

Working near Lake Merced, CA, in January 1941, a D-8 and Carryall scraper move sand to fill in a canyon.

Factory photo of early D-8 tractor with 8S hydraulic dozer.

Working near Baltimore, MD in 1939, a D-8 tractor and Letourneau Carryall handles 1500 - 1800 yards of material per day, working on the Governor Ritchie Highway.

Two side boom equipped D-8 pipe layers work together on an Oklahoma pipe line job.

BIG JOBS
ARE AHEAD

A lot of fine words have been written about the big tractor-bulldozers and the tough tasks they have handled in this war. Manned by Engineers and Seabees, they have spearheaded invasion landings—hauled supplies and equipment ashore—smashed enemy pillboxes—opened trails for troops—built roads across tropic swamps and Arctic tundra—slashed airfields out of the jungle.

War correspondents have "discovered" the husky machines and turned the spotlight on them. Actually, those same "Caterpillar" Diesels had been slugging it out with equally tough jobs long before Pearl Harbor. They've taken the military tasks in their stride.

Leaving out the grimness and the glamour of war, the toughest tractor jobs in the world are peacetime jobs. And there'll be plenty of them to be licked in the years ahead.

No mountain grade is so steep, no desert so torrid, no polar waste so cold, but that one day man will find work to do there. Once started, such undertakings must be fought through, with no quarter asked or given.

"Caterpillar" Diesels are a match for those jobs. When the war is over, there will be more of them than ever before, time-tried and battle-proved, ready to resume the work for which they were built—the tough, profitable, never-ending tasks of peace.

CATERPILLAR TRACTOR CO. • PEORIA, ILLINOIS

CATERPILLAR
DIESEL
ENGINES • TRACTORS
MOTOR GRADERS
EARTHMOVING EQUIPMENT

1940's vintage Caterpillar magazine advertisement featuring D-8 tractors equipped with Letourneau blades and scrapers.

RD-8 fitted with canopy and brush rake works near Villa, TX, April 1938.

Factory photo of a later model D-8 with 8A dozer.

Factory photo of a 7 roller later model D-8, direct drive.

A later model D-8 equipped with 8A hydraulic dozer and front mounted pump.

3744

Factory photo of a later model D-8 showing 7 roller track frames and rock guard removed, and rear mounted single shank hydraulic ripper.

Santiam Lumber Company of Sweet Home, OR, uses a D-8 tractor equipped with 8S bulldozer and Hyster winch to skid logs to a landing near Foster, OR.

A 14A D-8 with fully enclosed canopy and 8A dozer uses a Hyster winch to skid logs to a Washington landing.

Factory photo of D-8 tractor series F, also known as a 14A.

A later model D-8 with 8U hydraulic dozer is shown in a factory photo.

D-8 equipped with fully enclosed cab, front bumper and lights for either forestry or winter work.

July 1965. A D-8H with #128 rear double drum cable control is shown in a factory photo.

D-8 with cab and rear mounted hydraulic unit pulls five 7' seed drills. Carter, WA, 1956.

Factory photo of a 3 shank #8 ripper installed on a later model direct drive D-8.

Factory photo of D-8 equipped with 8A dozer and front mounted cable control.

September 11, 1964. A D-8H is shown equipped with an 8A cable controlled bulldozer.

November 21, 1963. Front view of a D-8 tractor equipped with 8S bulldozer.

January 9, 1964. Factory photo of a D-8H with a 7 roller track frame.

Two later model D-8s work along side a D-9 in a company publicity photo.

Factory photo of a D-8H equipped with 8S dozer and rear mounted cable control unit.

D-8H shown in a factory photo with a straight blade with inside arms and rear cable control unit. This blade was commonly used on tractors that push loaded scrapers.

Factory photo of later model D-8 equipped with 8S dozer and front mounted cable control.

A D-8 tractor and #80 scraper work in the cut on a California construction site.

Factory photo of a later model D-8 equipped with 8S hydraulic dozer and a front mounted pump.

D-8 direct drive tractor equipped with #8 ripper as shown in a factory photo.

Factory photo of a later model D-8 equipped with 8U dozer and front mounted cable control unit.

November 7, 1968. A power shift D-8H equipped with an 8S bulldozer and 183B hydraulic control.

Rear view of D-8H.

A late model D-8 with rear mounted cable laying machine cuts a trench in a California field.

January 23, 1964. Side view of D-8H direct drive.

November 8, 1968. Direct drive D-8H model view.

114

February 23, 1971. Power shift D-8H with 7 roller track frame.

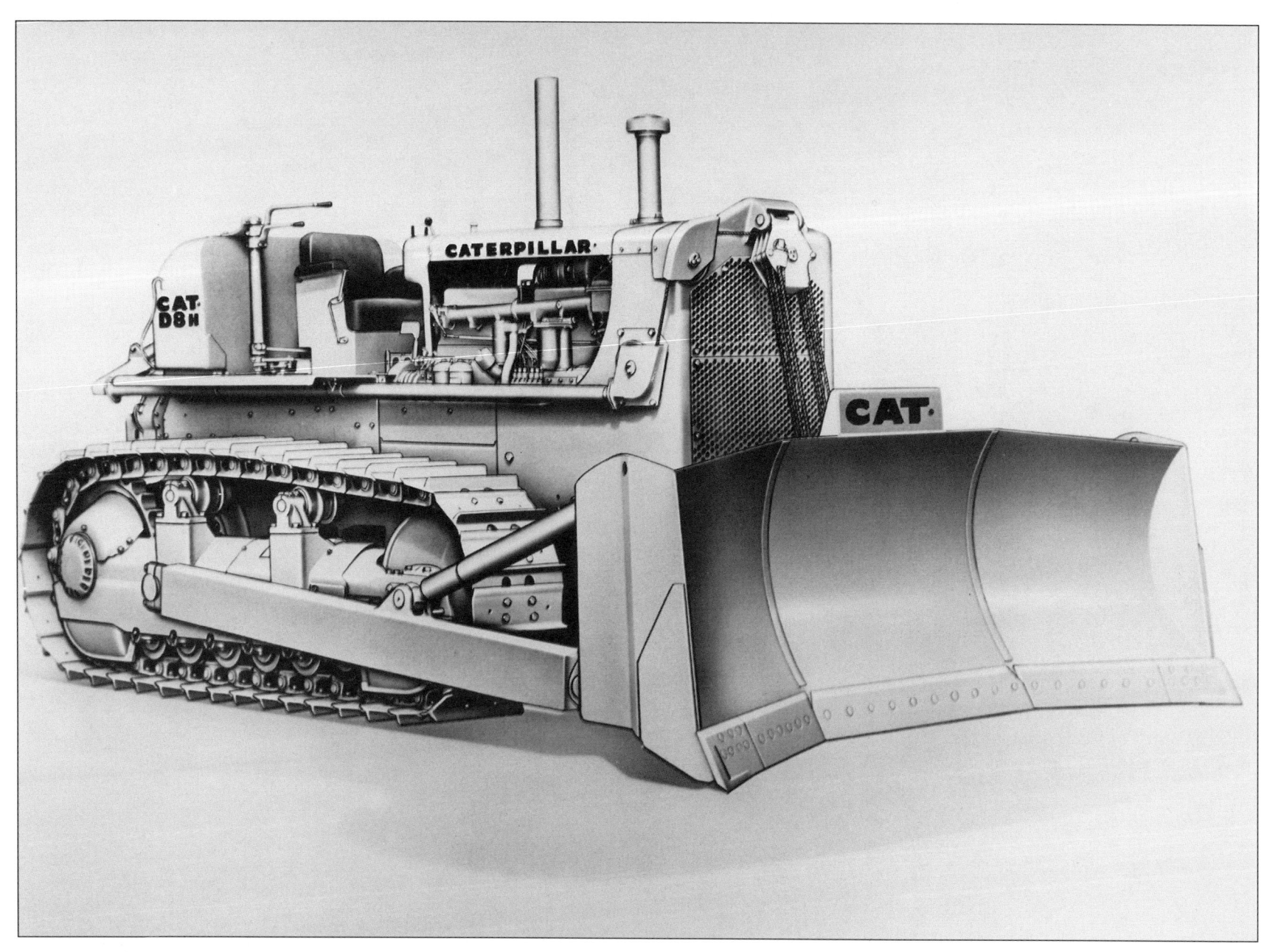

D-8H equipped with 8U dozer and rear mounted cable control unit.

Direct drive D-8 tractor with rock guard cut-away, showing 7 roller track frame.

D-8H direct drive with 6 bottom rollers, as shown in a factory photo.

An earlier model D-8 2U with rear mounted cable control unit works to fill low ground in Northern Minnesota.

October 1, 1963. Factory photo shows the rear mounted single shank ripper on the D-8H.

43988

November 8, 1968, a factory photo of the power shift of the D-8H.

Factory photo of later model D-8 direct drive tractor with cut-away showing 6 roller track frame.

A 2U D-8 with rear mounted cable control unit opens the apron and ejects the load on a #80 scraper.

Factory photo taken November 7, 1968, showing the D-8H with the 8C hydraulic bulldozer.

Side profile of the Caterpillar D-8K.

Growing Time

This spring, all across the land, you'll see husky "Caterpillar" Diesel Tractors and their matched earthmoving equipment building new roads—widening and improving old ones. This is important to the whole nation. It's important to *you*. For roads decrease distances, expand markets, bring people together oftener and in greater numbers. "Caterpillar" builds the power that helps the country grow.

CATERPILLAR TRACTOR CO., PEORIA, ILL.

CATERPILLAR DIESEL
REG. U. S. PAT. OFF.

WHEN YOU THINK OF
BETTER HIGHWAYS, THINK OF THE
BIG YELLOW MACHINES THAT BUILD THEM

ENGINES
TRACTORS
MOTOR GRADERS
EARTHMOVING EQUIPMENT

A D-8 and #80 pan unload fill in a 1940's advertisement. When the apron is lifted completely open the ejector moves ahead, pushing out the material.

More Titles from Iconografix:

*This product is sold under license from Mack Trucks, Inc. Mack is a registered Trademark of Mack Trucks, Inc. All rights reserved.

All Iconografix books are available from direct mail specialty book dealers and bookstores worldwide, or can be ordered from the publisher. For book trade and distribution information or to add your name to our mailing list contact

Iconografix   Telephone: (715) 381-9755
PO Box 446   (800) 289-3504 (USA)
Hudson, Wisconsin, 54016   Fax: (715) 381-9756

CATERPILLAR MILITARY TRACTORS VOL. 1
PHOTO ARCHIVE

CATERPILLAR MILITARY TRACTORS VOL. 2
PHOTO ARCHIVE

MORE GREAT BOOKS FROM ICONOGRAFIX

CATERPILLAR MILITARY TRACTORS VOLUME 1
ISBN 1-882256-16-6

CATERPILLAR SIXTY
ISBN 1-882256-05-0

CATERPILLAR MILITARY TRACTORS VOLUME 2
ISBN 1-882256-17-4

HOLT TRACTORS
ISBN 1-882256-10-7

RUSSELL GRADERS
ISBN 1-882256-11-5

CATERPILLAR *Photo Gallery*
ISBN 1-882256-70-0

CATERPILLAR D-2
ISBN 1-882256-99-9

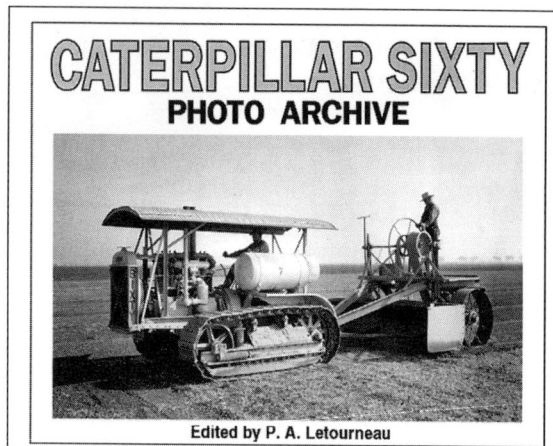

CATERPILLAR SIXTY
PHOTO ARCHIVE

Edited by P. A. Letourneau

HOLT TRACTORS
PHOTO ARCHIVE

Edited by P. A. Letourneau

CATERPILLAR
PHOTO GALLERY

Edited by P. A. Letourneau

RUSSELL GRADERS
PHOTO ARCHIVE

Edited by P. A. Letourneau

CATERPILLAR D-2 & R-2
PHOTO ARCHIVE

Bob LaVoie